MAUREEN FITZPATRICK
BOOKS

Beyond Horizon Fall

*The poetic journey of an
addict's mom
(second edition)*

**Maureen Alexandra
Fitzpatrick**

Beyond Horizon Fall
Written and arranged by
Maureen Alexandra Fitzpatrick

Cover art by
**Mary Kate
Fitzpatrick** and
Maureen Fitzpatrick

Please feel free to contact me with any questions or comments at
www.souljargon.com

Follow me on facebook at
Maureen Alexandra

Instagram at **scarletspoem**

Tumblr at **mauralex**

Twitter at **mauralex**

Wordpress at **Writinglass**

This book is dedicated to the countless beautiful, strong, and resilient families who are engaged in a life or death struggle with a loved one. May you find peace in the knowledge that you are not alone nor to blame. And may you find hope and strength in these words.

I encourage you to write your own thoughts in the space provided at the end of this book.
Try it, you may find a bit of healing there.

Contents

The Beginning: Despair

The day you were born
I cried happy tears

Prize

There is no greater love
than the bond between
mother and daughter,
father and son,
at least for awhile.
I never knew the devil had
a bond stronger,
a hypnotic prize just for
you.
And so a new relationship
began,
A blossoming love,
becoming all consuming,
And I was cast aside.

Safety

This little child with hair
of gold,
so full of life, story untold.
Her pain misunderstood,
confusing her mom,
lost in the abyss,
walls too high to climb.

Find my hand child,
I need saving too.

*They'll say the devil
made you do it;
I'd have to agree*

The Devil's Dance

A rabid dance

Between mother and child

Daughter and drug

Writhing
Swirling
Twisting

Violent efforts to shake

The devil's music

From her soul

Where are you my child?
Please
Return to me

A Break

The enormity of this world
in which I sleep
Overwhelms me

Chirping crickets and
foraging bears
Intrigue me

Gentle breeze
Rustling leaves
Sooth me

Thoughts of you alone
Somewhere
Terrify me

Goodnight, my love
I miss you

Chains

Chains of burden, shame,
and guilt
Strapped to her chest
Trudging up hill

There she climbs a drug
filled cliff
Her body weary, in need
of rest

Take the ropes and hold
on tight
I'll pull you in, make it
alright

*I heard you crying
somewhere*

Today

Today is hard.
I've no idea where you
are, why you left; and you
have no idea that your
actions are causing my
spirit to shatter, my soul to
die, my hope to diminish
and my life to crumble.
How dare you!

Just for a moment
I close my eyes and let sleep
wash over me.
I pray sometimes that I don't
wake up.

The Feast

Devil's keeper walking,
Prince of Darkness
stalking, machetes in their
mitts.
Duck, my love.
Their life is nourished by
your fear, and they will
steal extra rations if you let
them.
Steer them away from
your smorgasbord, for
they seek shelter under
gray aura. And they will
wait, and stalk, and
pounce ravenously,
anxious to destroy your
strength with their
weapons, desperate to
drink your blood until you
die a quiet, woeful death.
Run to me, let me help. I'm
wearing steel toed boots
and will kick them hard in
the shins. Then maybe,
just maybe, you might find
a bit of peace.

Howling Wind

Allow me to follow your
woeful song.
Screeching wind bristles at
my ears.

I see her there, head
nodding, chin glistening,
spittle
dribbling.

I'm scared.
I didn't think eyes could
roll back any further.

She scratches.
Scabs of yesterday become
scars of tomorrow; the
picking never ceases.

Locked behind the
bathroom door, one hour,
two hours, three hours, till
I bust the damn thing
down, only to sit her next
to me and watch her head
fall to dented Formica.
Again, the hospitals won't
keep her. They never do.
What the hell???

Dammit. The sound of the
howling wind refuses to
cease.

I'm only a little glad you're
home. Life is easier when I
don't have to watch you die.

Bullshit

Sometimes I wonder
where I am, if I am real, if
there really is a shiny blue
sky above me. So often it
feels like an impossibility
to feel something other
than grief, a futility to
believe in hope and pretty
pink flowers. I look
around and I see it, but all
I feel is the evil fertilizing
our kids, the chemical
bullshit masquerading as
peace.

*I'm feeling broken like
shattered glass. Please make
the glue to fix it invisible.
I don't want more scars.*

The Game

Dangle my heart over a
cliff; you may as well set it
adrift,
amongst the septic souls
with whom you allow, to
steal your soul after you
took a vow,
To stay away!
To push away!
the very devil that stole
your life,
and set me afloat in a
world of strife,
of hopelessness and torrid
pain,
and now I may never see
you again.
You've lost yourself to the
monster of drugs,
and I've lost myself to the
push and shove,
of playing my cards to
help you survive.
I've lost the game,
it won you, but I've died.

The Crown

She slumps in a crack
house
Dead eyes cast down
Riches stolen from loved
ones
Buy a rat feces crown
Lonely, despondent, filthy
and sick, open sores ooze
lost hope, danger lurks
with each trick
Her life was once vibrant
Now I'm afraid death
might win
My daughter's a stranger,
Fuck heroin!

Allow me to lead you to
greener pasture,
Come,
take my hand

Black Hole

And finally the day came,
Dead pall falls
Covering hope's mercy
With doubt's midnight
hell,
A black hole epiphany,
A remembrance revisited.

Trophies

Trying to sleep during a
waking nightmare is fun,
A pessimistic game of who
will win: the monstrous
pain or slumber?
I saw pain's shelves the
other day
filled to the brim with
trophies.

Boom

What if the world ended, a
big boom explosion,
rupturing deities,
detonating personal
assumption,
not from a nuke or ISIS,
but from the malevolent
energy of our souls,
disconnected through
distrust and hurt, envy
and sadness?
What if all that was left
was suspended in time? A
spiritual ghost of what
could have been, had we
not tossed personal filth
towards the prosperity of
others. Imagine if all that
was left was nothing.
Love. Just love.

Bricks

The first brick went up.

"I refuse to go to school today."

The second brick went up.

"I don't have to listen to you!"

The third brick went up.

"I hope you fucking die!"

The fourth brick went up.

"Your daughter seems fine. We are sending her home from the ER."

The fifth brick went up.

"She's your problem, lady!"

The sixth brick went up.

"Please come home and help me with her now!!"

The seventh brick went
up.

"This is CBS news
reporting a missing girl."

The eighth brick went up.

"My daughter threw her
body though my picture
window. I want her
arrested!"

The ninth brick went up.

"Your child is being
arrested for burglary."

The tenth brick went up.

"HIPAA laws allow her
to leave this hospital if she
chooses."

The eleventh brick went
up.

"But she's only 16, and
she's sick!!"

The twelfth brick went up.

"Lady, I can't put her in rehab if she doesn't want to go. I don't care if you're her mother."

The last brick went up.

"My kid would never do that. Where are her parents?"

The truth is, I was here all along, fighting for my child from behind this massive brick wall.

Do you know I've heard people say we should have been better parents? Fuck them. How do you explain addiction to those with their heads buried in sand?

Maybe

I've dreams still, heroin's
ugly face chasing you,
razor teethed fear biting
down on you, on me.
The beginning: Teenaged
awkward loneliness, bat-
whacked self esteem,
Mt. St. Helen's
combustible anger
combining, erupting,
pouring forth tear filled
lava, trapping your beauty
underneath, to suffocate,
drown, in the hot turmoil
of an executioner's plan.
For heroin only has one
goal dear, to kill; to smile
as a parent buries their
very soul along with their
child, joining thousands
of other varsity letter
holders, high school band
leaders, softball pitchers,
and beautiful geeks deep
inside maggot filled, body
rotting earth.....eternally.
If only you knew your
worth. If only I had held
you more. If only every
God forsaken drug dealer
could step into a parent's

nightmare for even a few
seconds and truly feel the
torturous, helpless,
grinding, rip your heart
out raw, no anesthesia,
unbearable dagger of that
five buck devil. If only....
Then maybe, just maybe
you'd be ok.

Solace

I think back at times

And my body becomes

a vibrating base

Pouring dark

reverberations

deep into my soul

Causing me to stop

breathing

Inviting panic in

as the slow, low pitched

music plays

the Bogey Man's theme

song

And I pray for release

Solace

More time in between

To forget

To forgive

To live

To love

Faith doesn't sleep with me anymore. Distrust and anger do. Faith is for those who believe in magic. I prefer to believe in you.

Faith

They tell me to believe, to
find faith, as if it were a
simple child's bouncy ball
lost under thick brush.
"How can you live
without faith?" they ask.
I ask, "How can I live with
it?" You see, I had it once,
at least a miniscule dose,
when I prayed for healing
from a summer's cold or
stomach cramps. But I
knew they'd heal anyway,
with or without religion.
But when I put my faith in
Him when I needed it
most, comfort and relief
from the mental storm
raging within you, my
child, I found none. Night
after night the storm
raged, rearing its ugly
head more vehemently
each episode, and the little
faith I had, fell to the
tempest. Yes, it is easier to
live without God, for then
the disillusionment and
abandonment don't hurt
quite so much. No

expectations....no
disappointment.

*I wish you'd open the
bathroom door.
I can't stand the thought of
breaking down another door,
yet I can't stand the thought
of not.*

I've No Rights

I thought you'd be smarter
with hiding it. I guess
you're now at the point
you just don't care. There
are tinfoil pieces and burnt
spoons everywhere; there
are shoelaces and little
baggies all over the house.
With all this evidence and
your rolled back eyes and
needle marks, I still can't
get you into rehab
BECAUSE YOU REFUSE.
Where are my parental
rights?

Heroin's Nightmare
A Poem by Her

"Ping"
The elevator glides open
"Wait," I think to myself.
"This can't be right." I step
out into total darkness, the
sound of my footsteps all
that echoes through the
still. I look around,
bewildered, confused, but
curious. Suddenly there's
a flickering of light in the
distance. I'm captivated.
It's enchanting. A sense of
glory and warmth pour
over me as I make my way
to its beauty. The darkness
is now just background
noise. The simplicity of the
light casts away the terrors
of the night. I start
running, my excitement
getting the best of my will.
Running, running, run!
Something is wrong. What
is taking so long? Why
haven't I reached my
flame? Panic sets in. The
beauty of the light fades,
and the more I run, the

further it is. The knots in
my chest are churning.
The flame is dimming and
the heat is rising.
Then…blackness.
Whoosh!! I know I am not
alone. I feel the demon's
breath. Choking on ash, I
try to catch my breath,
trying to catch my
thoughts as they dash by
hundreds of miles per
hour. My breath shortens,
each attempt to breathe
stopped by the knots in
my stomach until they are
held captive for good. The
room starts spinning,
shaking, spiraling down.
Slam!
I sit up in a haze, the black
now grey. All that is light
and all that is dark become
one. No emotion, no
concern, just wandering.

*You surprise me with your
intelligence.
Don't give it to the demons.
Use it for good.*

Crazy Me

I'm crouching like the

girl in the crazy movies,

in a corner, head down,

shaking, crying,

screaming, scared I

might stay here forever.

It's the only place I feel

safe today.

*Carry me, Lord, as you carry
her too.
But if we get too heavy,
Please lay me down and just
carry her.*

Sad Life

Phone confiscated
Money lost
Car towed
Overload

Boyfriend booked
Purse stolen
Key inside
Pimp a ride

No entrance
All alone
Standing small
Gonna fall

Sad soul
Yes, my dear
Drugs suck
I give a fuck

Lost mind
Too bad
You did this
You took the risk

Beg a pass
For the bus
Grab a cup
Toughen up

Then check into
Rehab please
Before you die
And make me cry

*Are you thinking today that
you'd finally like to get
better?
Or will you once again tell me
you like living in the flea bag
motel with a drugged up
stranger, pissy shit mattress,
and
rotten smelly God knows
what?*

Rescue Me

I awaken again to
nothingness,
to invisibleness,
the lonely echo of my own
breathing,
pounding me,
raping me,
crushing me
under the weight of
phantom woe,
every thrust pushing me
further and deeper
into restless hell.
And as the new day
breaks,
I hear the love songs of
birds,
and I reach out my hand
offering my soul
to the beauty outside my
barren chamber,
and I pray
that someone, somewhere,
feels my hungry plea for
respite,
and will rescue me
from this infertile assault
and pull me safely into the
comfort of their arms.

Your brother vomited in my car today. You know, because we raced outside to escape your drug fueled violence. I love you, child, but this can't go on.

Hope

We murmur of forever

Of life lived fully

Dancing on the precipice
of now and then

Soon and never

Waltzing back and forth

Here and there

Singing happy songs as we
tumble on black leather

Giggling

Unsure but not unaware

That this time is precious

Rare

And that whispered hopes
and cha chas

Give lyrical context

To the meaning of family

The swirls are the worst
The unsteady, shaky whirling
that rarely ceases.
They say it's anxiety,
but I know it's fear.

Walking Away

She asked me to die today.

"Fuck you, fuck you, die!"

-Because I love her and
can't help her anymore,
until she helps herself-

My beautiful princess,
waiting in her dungeon to
be rescued.

But I choose to turn away,

And walk towards the
pretty fields of green.

Fuck me
Fuck me

I think I have died

Hitherland

Hitherland they wail

Empty trumpets

Desperate sounds

They sing in solitary

Confinement

Theirs alone

If I keep up this crying
We will all die together
In a river of tears

Fairy Tale Faith

Splintery wooden prayers
unanswered,
I was down on my knees
for you, Lord.
Where the hell were you?
I cried tears I never knew I
had.
Shiny-pew church dreams
shattered as you turned
your back on my pain, on
hers.
Good Lord, God.
Who and where are you?
Do you exist, or is the
fairy tale faith I had just
that,

a fairy tale?

Beast

Somewhere in the night
lives the beast of prey,
feeding on the last vibrant
droplets of dreams from
the downtrodden, his
fangs carefully poised and
ready to pounce when
another leaden step
stumbles, falls. His
hunger, an angry monster
of empty promise, a barren
chamber of acidic need,
will follow you into the
path of gory uncertainty, a
place to maim, a place to
kill.
The gloom has come, hope
is now buried beneath
treacherous longing. Fear
is your new friend, a
gentle caress of warning.
Heed her. Run, baby, run.

Empty

Hollow echoes of despair
toss silent sounds of
futility
'round and 'round and
'round.

It's empty in there.

Black nihility filled with
spacious nothingness
surrounds in chill's forlorn
grip. Welcome to the death
of something that was.

It's empty in there.

Like the prosperity of
Gospel or the starving
gullet of lone Siberian
lemmings,

It's empty in there.

Such is my heart:
Bared, naked, and void of
feeling.
That's what the blue bag
does to a mom.

Get well, so I don't have to
stay......

empty in there.

*I often wonder about
the dog shows. I thought
allowing you to travel would
do you good, allow you to
find a bit of peace in your
cyclonic mind. Maybe I was
wrong.*

Deceit

Medals and honors and
fancy wins

I see dogs, snarling

They wear deceit in their
coats and manipulation in
their tails

Claws scratch the shiny
surfaces

You smile as you prance
with them

They smile as they grant
you another victory

And as they sniff, so do
you.

Gods

Matted, curly hair gods
walk around town.
How I sometimes pray
murder were legal.
They float above the
sidewalks
out on bail again.
And they flaunt their
power, their Houdini
magic,
free again from iron bars,
"Smile people. We are
back.
Nothing can get us. Lol,
lol, lol! "
A bullet would.
But there'd be no Houdini
breaks for me.
Somehow those matted,
curly headed gods always
win.
I hate them.

Funeral

Your funeral has
happened.
Words of wisdom have
been spoken to the crowd.
Tears have been cried and
songs sung.
They played your favorite
song.
We ate your favorite food.
We shared your favorite
stories.
And we cursed the drugs
that took your life.
Yes, you are still here,
But I've already been to
your funeral.

Someone

Jackass, scumbag

or is he?

I love you.

Someone must love him.

But why is he sitting in the
convenience store parking
lot in his rusted Chevy
waiting for you?

Jackass, scumbag

I followed you.

I caught him.

Put my Lincoln bumper
against his dilapidated
junker.

Told him to get the fuck
out of town, while praying
a bullet didn't cut my
thoughts.

Low life loser

He had to be 40.

I should have called the
cops.

Instead I played vigilante.

It kind of felt good.

I lived through it.

I hope he learned from it.

Lowlife, scum

*Yeah, not feeling too
charitable today.*

The Invader

It's a wonder this pain
doesn't kill, the way the
tired ego cries with each
dagger, defeated,
knotty black joylessness
alive with fury,
a woman held hostage,
scratching deep within,
clawing, clawing, clawing
her way out. Tonight I'll
open my window,
then my mouth,
hopeful that she will
disgorge herself through
the corroded cavities of
my being, leaving a bitter
aftertaste I can gargle
away from my soul.

B12

The dark pall suffocates.
Its evil essence stalls,
purposely, intent on
squeezing the last ounce of
air from my lungs.
I'm ready for a brawl, a
last fucking go; a test of
my b12.
Broken dreams are my
strength.
I think of all I've given
self-lessly. And in this
moment I wish I'd been
more selfish. For in the
end it doesn't matter.
"Fuck you," it mocks.
"Yes, fuck me," I answer.
At least we agree on that.

Putrid vomit expels itself
from the confines of my pith.
Rancid agony fills the air, it
smells,
I hurt.
Where the hell are you?

Days Like This

I hate when the punishable
thunder rumbles from
afar, damning my soul,
tearing chasms into the
very core of my being,
spilling the blood I had so
carefully saved for a day
my heart would truly need
to bleed for you.
Yes, I'm nothing now but
a casperous shell wishing
these past eight hours go
stuff themselves.
Hard.
My mama forgot to tell
me there'd be days like
this.

Emotions

I can't even explain to you
the emotions.
I'm feeling things I've never
felt before.
Have you ever watched a
horror movie and
had a temporary racing of the
heart and sense of
absolute dread that you
quickly
recover from once the scene
has passed?
Now imagine that feeling all
day, every day,
and at this point it has been
years.
Honestly, I can't believe I can
still function as a mom,
as a human being.
My stress level has got to
have out spilled stroke
territory.
Why am I here? I can
sometimes barely move?
Driving has become difficult
because of the constant panic.
I'm shaking and lightheaded
as I type this very passage.
Good God, help us all. Good
God, help her.

SOS

What am I really searching
for when the veil of
uncertainty waltzes
clumsily before me?
When one day I'm sure,
then at the next harbor,
doubtful?
Which lighthouse will
guide me home from
stormy turmoil, to grant
me peace, to gift me love's
precious shelter, to allow
me to once again feel the
simple silken sand as it
cascades gently between
my toes? To which beacon
of strength shall I crawl to
save myself from
drowning?

Refuse

Night comes too early
to those who wish for
light.
Selfish notions squeeze
away self indulgent
thoughts of misery's
contentment.
Frayed chord circles life's
uncertainty, dangling like
a noose around willful
breaths.
Pessimistic thoughts will
be hung tonight and
uncertainty left in the
gallows.
For though night will
surely come,
refuse to let the darkness
win,
refuse to bow to madness.

Door slams in stunned face,
drafting whiffs of Marlboros.
She thinks me a pest.

Soldiers

Sometimes there are just
too many pressures
advancing,
tin soldiers armed with
grenades.
"Ready, aim. Fire," they
yell.
Their taunts and blasts fire
deep into the core,
threatening to shake any
bit of peace currently
contained.
There's always one bomb
that stings like hell,
burning into self's center
and tearing up the soul.
Nothing hurts more than
unexpected explosions in
carefully guarded hearts.

Corpse

Earthy marrow coats
paper thin epidermis.
Minuscule droppings mix
with the decaying skin.
I'm six feet under
listening to the pounding
rain above,
hoping for a dribble,
a bit of liquid life.
But the only life I feel is
the maggots making love
to the decaying corpse
called me.

I hate jagged edges.
They cut.
I hate drugs.
They have jagged edges.

I Don't Like Him

Your friend Stefan was
surely swell.
Love the guy.
Such a beautiful and
giving soul to introduce
you to drugs,
such a trusting and loyal
friend to stay by your side
during your arrests and
incarcerations and
disappearances and near
overdoses.
Yes, Stefan is such a loyal
friend. For who else would
be there after all those
trials to give you a little
more of this or that to get
you through? Such a
beautiful gift.
Such a beautiful giver.
Ugh.

His Name Is Drug

I've been swindled by the
drug too. Not in the way
you have. You see, I never
took him, never would
think about taking him,
but he still fooled me. He
made me believe your lies
so many times I can't
count. He led me into
naivety, when I should
have known better. He
shook me down for fear of
his violence so much, that
I retreated rather than
stood. He held me
hostage, when I should
have been
strong.
He almost killed me
and my family,
and I almost let him.
I always thought I was
strong.
Apparently, I'm not.

Panic at My Disco

I feel the cascading tears,
liquid marbles tracing,
following the labyrinth of
206 marrowed bones,
paths of strength.
They say jittery skeletons
are not real. They live only
in the dark crevices of the
desperate underworld,
aching to be realized. But
I see them.
I feel them.
I am them.
I hang desperate, noosed
and gasping for air.

Rattle, rattle, roll, gasp!

What is that sound but the
dark destitution of
loneliness,
an anxiety filled display of
unselfish talent?
Percussion at its finest.
Jittery bones jitter and
quake.
Drum roll please!

Tum, tum, tum!

Beautiful music of a fearful
soul.
Devil's delight.
Let's dance with our
thorns upon our head,
spirit half dead.
Lonely symphony crying,
spirit of one dying.
Don't tell me it's all in my
head. Just take a look.
You will see my dread.
Panic lives, panic sings.

Rattle, rattle, roll.

*Had I known this life would
have me carry the tormented
anchor of a thousand
suffering souls, I might have
taken a detour.*

Rain

And so it rains…
Dripping drops of muddy
grey,
falling razor sharp
through the smoky mists
of sorrow,
sharp and cutting into her
brave skin,
emitting wafts of rancid
iron
and wailing crimson,
tides of an unfair world.

She stands there naked,
exposed, and proud,
a stalwart sacrificial lamb,
beautifully tragic,
a lone creature amongst
greedy dealers,
giving her last shards of
heartfelt fortitude to the
wind.
The rain whips.
The rain wallops.
And so she bleeds.
Good God, have mercy.

River

I'll cry a thousand tears
from the lonesome
confines of my head,
Create the perfect river,
I'll go floating there
instead.
I'll look for someone there
to glide down salty and
free,
Holding hands together,
I hope it's you and me.

*Can't you just go on a heroin
diet? Just don't use it. I'll do
it with you, but I'll give up
chocolate. I promise. Let's do
this together.*

Lollipops

Sometimes in life
everything sucks

You try to be what
everyone wants

but still everything sucks

You give 10,000% of your
soul

but still everything sucks

Give me a thousand
popsicles and ten
thousand lollipops

I'll make it real

I'll make sure

everything sucks

I just can't face life today.

Cannon

I just realized,
I am a loose cannon.
Maybe that's better than
that stiff board part of me.
Perhaps I will use the
cannon to break the board,
to make a tent where I can
meditate and relax so my
cannon doesn't fire so
impulsively again.
Hmm, there's an idea.

I know I'm goofy sometimes,
but it's for fun, to lighten life.
Did I embarrass you? Ugh, I
hope not.

Hope's Death

Perhaps it's a blessing.
Hope's last will was
written up in winter news,
a clear indication that she
had at last died. Never
again will the August
flame of a perfect soul
shine down upon her
innocence, allowing a little
bit of light to reach her
broken heart, or to set her
amber tresses aglow. As
eulogies go, it was a good
one, an outline of once
was, including her faith in
yesteryear's promise and
her triumphs so many
years ago over the evil tug
of pessimism. Yes, hope
has died. The constant
barrage of words used as
ammunition, shot in tiny
bursts into her soul,
chipping away at
whatever health she could
hold onto, finally killing
her. The disease of a self
loathing, self centered
world tore the last bits of
her in two, leaving a path
of bloody entrails, a final

gift to the filthy varmint of
the world, oh so happy to
feast once more.
Hope,
may she finally rest in
peace.

He's a good man, your dad,
strong, but your friend heroin
is killing him,
killing us.
Our hands are being torn
apart,
our hearts barely holding
onto this tether of despair.

Hell

Just how far down is hell,

six feet or sixty million?

Human furnace,

wafts of ribs barbecued

in solidarity or maybe

solitary, had the deeds

pursued living

outweighed in

repugnance those of

another. And if I should

die before I wake and

head to hell my soul to

take, I wish to find an

inglenook, sixty million

feet down, to hide for

just a moment, before

the fiery pit of Abaddon

makes me scream for

mercy as my tears of rue

and regret dance

upward in pretty swirls,

steamy ribbons of death,

to bless the living with

my mournful gift, my

debt of compunction, a

chilly morning fog.

Make Me a Tree

This paper, my heart, two
halves, ink black

This life, this love,
this drug, so smug

My words, her words,
these fights, our poem

Then rip, then tear,
my paper, her hair

My words, they fall,
get trampled, then stall

In mud, my sonnet
Her rage, her comet

My life, this page,
Debris, thrown away

I can't reach her, she left
I'm once again, bereft

This paper, this poem our
song, long gone

I wish I were a tree

*I was working at a new job
when you called
threatening to kill yourself.
I started to panic in a room
full of sixth graders.
I had to run home from that
new job repeatedly. I'm
surprised they didn't send me
packing.*

Shaky

I still get shaky.
A lot.
When I type or drive.
I might even get heart
palpitations and a light
head.
The reaction is always the
same,
panic in one form or
another,
over a trip to a restaurant,
or a harp lesson,
or a baseball game.
"Boo, I'm still here!" panic
tells me.
I had hoped him gone.
But he rides along in the
car, sneaks into my purse,
follows me to the shower,
wants to take over my
shadow, I believe.
That fear,
that unbelievable emotion
of dread,
that haunting overflow of
hopelessness is here sitting
next to me.
Still.
I wish I could just swat
him away.

Threads of intestine, knots of
gore, tie me up daily. Rotten
brain pleas don't help. When
a soul starts to die, begging
help from a sick body falls on
deaf ears.

Beseech

I beseech thee, oh heart, to
allow me a moment's
peace,
to banter with my restless
brain,
to implore it to forget
love's dying hold.
Allow me a restful
slumber curled up with
my grandma's quilt,
fluffy socks and humming
rain,
to rock my aching soul
gently away from
incessant thoughts of her
dying grace,
her joyless song.

Resurrection

Last week the knots in my
stomach threatened to
break and bleed me out,
until my corpse descended
gracefully over the
crumbed up linoleum of
the kitchen floor.
And yes, yesterday was
better, thanks to an
ongoing dizzy spell
warping my mind, and a
gaggle of silly teens
running about,
but today hurts once more;
tear producing, heart
shattering, tummy
spasming bad.
Though if my hollow
corpse could fall and rise
once already, perhaps it's
not out of divine
resurrections.

Our Cups Runneth Over

God only gives us what
we can handle. It's the nice
people's way of saying,
we've no choice but to
deal with the cards we've
been dealt. Short of
suicide, truly what choice
do we have? Who decides
our capacity for anything,
our ability to fill up our
stress cups before they
runneth over? Or do we
have multiple stress cups?
Maybe a shot glass for
work shit and a tumbler
for kid shit, green, with
middle fingers pointing
towards the heavens.
We've each a capacity to
do more than we've ever
imagined. In simplest
form, it's shown with the
millions of people who
awaken each day and
head, robotic like, to jobs
that slowly tear them
apart; a big, green cup
chewing machine, creating
cracks, and painting wear,

but never allowing the true measure of our capacity to reach its rim. Maybe the bits of stress that leak through the fissures grant us more time before we overflow, before we jump off that bridge, use that gun, or twist from the pain of madness. But then there are the family problems, the other problems. I can imagine internal boxes slowly being filled. Dad and Mom don't get along, Sarah uses drugs, Joey has cancer, Suzy is a klepto, Daddy fooled around. How much can one person take? How many tons of Xanax and Paxil and Zoloft will be dispensed? Just dump it in the damned water; we all need it. How many gyms will gain memberships with those looking to de-stress, only to lose them because people are too stressed to get there? Yes, we all have our little boxes, our shot glasses, our green, fuck

you tumblers within. But
look around. I see too
many of them
overflowing, their stench
and poison reaching those
left still half full. God
didn't give everyone the
ability to handle their
portion of difficulty.
Unfortunately.

I think he gave me way too
much. I'm not happy with
HIM right now.

Feelings

Carefully manicured
feelings tumble down,
and the big bad queen
found me hiding.
Not sure why I feel the
need to run,
to shroud myself from
something.
I feel like I'm holding the
poison apple and I'm
supposed to take a bite.

Bitterness and anger
continue to swell in tidal
waves.
Bring a wave of peace soon,
so I'm not left wondering
when I will be washed away
for good.

Really Miley?

I see Miley sing of
partying with Mollies.
What's she thinking; that
it's safe? Harmless? Fun
jollies?

Free speech some might
say, but I say bullshit to
that. She's not just
singing, she's luring
others, that brat.

Has she seen what these
drugs have done
to families like mine?
Taken bright solid minds
and blown them up fine?

Not to mention the pain
put on my child's siblings
and me,
and the thousands of
dollars spent to set her
mind free.

The violent episodes when
drugs fueled her rage,
the cops, the neighbors,
and siblings her stage.

Gave me PTSD, yes, it's
true from that shit.
What the drugs did to her,
to me harder they hit.

For those of you thinking
just once might be fun,
that's all it takes, my
advice is to run.

Your skin will scab over.
Your soul will be bare.
You will end up dead.
Who can visit you there?

Don't think for a second,
"It will not be me."
The honest truth is,
neither did she.

Her love for her family has
been replaced,
by a false love for drugs,
yes, pills took our place.

Straight A student, star
pitcher she was,
Until her life went awry,
once she got her buzz.

Now she's missing
somewhere, and she's up
to bad strife.
And I'm hoping this
message can help save
your life.

*Yeah, I don't care for your
message, Miley.*

Wine Fog

By another daughter, her
sibling, Mary Kate

Wine fogged memories
become so clear.

I taste copper in my mouth
and realize it is blood from
biting my tongue for so
long.

I remember, God, I
remember.

And I sob because I don't
want to.

It's so easy to forget,
to pretend to forget, bottle
up my tears and sell them
as witch's potion,
Put a label on and call it
"Passive aggressive
heartbreak."

I loved you, and you
broke me.
And through awkward
phone calls and forced
laughs we try to come
back, because it hurts even

more to imagine this pain
as permanent.

*Your siblings love you; they
just can't show it right now.
Someday they will. A child's
heart breaks like the fragile,
crystal spun sugar of fairies.
Get better and show them
your true self. Then all that
sweet sugar will come your
way.*

Crystals

Another by Mary Kate, my
daughter, her sibling

There is no easy way to
describe the exact way a
heart can break. Mine
broke slowly, so much that
I didn't even notice, so
much beyond repair that I
still haven't figured out
quite how to fix it. I think
it was the first time I saw
Mom cry, how broken
you'd made her;
that was the first shard of
glass that cut me, though
there were so many
scattered across the floor
from your violent rage. It
felt like they were
embedded beneath my
skin, absorbed by my
blood, until I could not
remember how it felt to be
alive without constant
pain flowing within me.
I can still feel the shards,
though you've tried to
clean them up. Year after
year you get better at
sweeping them under the

rug; I guess you forget the
ones I've swallowed, the
sadness that still lives
within me. My heart broke
in small ways: everyday
that I could not fix you,
everyday that you lost
yourself in an even deeper
pain
that none of us could
understand. I do not
pretend to forgive you for
all you've done, but I will
say this: In certain lights,
broken glass can look like
crystals, and sometimes,
when you look long
enough they sparkle like
God.

Thai Food

Another by Miss Mary Kate

We talk over exotic spices
and foreign languages
until the room is as warm
and comforting as the
bottle of Merlot on the
table. Your wine stained
lips, so sweet, speak of
things so terrible that
you've endured, and I try
not to cry because I know
it embarrasses you. You
tell me of love turning to
ashen dust in your hands
and wayward children led
astray by evils we don't
understand,
of rose tinted dreams
dissipating under the
merciless tide of life, and
of prayers unanswered by
some kind of cruel God.
As you speak your eyes
replay the horrors of a
tragic past, and I can feel
the pain as they shield
behind blue armor the
same color as the skies of a
heaven you don't believe
in anymore. I fail in the
attempt to stifle my tears,

because I remember
thinking I had never seen
a woman more beautiful
and broken, that nothing
happens for a reason,
because it would be some
kind of a fucked up God to
allow the very flesh and
blood of a woman to
damage her so completely.
Perhaps it is some kind of
blood sacrifice needed, a
pagan God of such, thirsty
for the blood of the
innocent.
I do not understand why
bad things happen to good
people and why such good
intentions pave the road to
hell. All I know is that you
are the most wonderful
woman I have ever met,
and on nights when there
is static stillness and I lay
my head across your lap, I
cannot feel your jagged
edges, only the soft sound
of constant love.

Love is funny.
We are supposed to love
unconditionally. I suppose I
do, however, when the devil
attacks, I second guess that
"given."

Bad Maps

I don't know what you are
thinking;
I don't understand how
you got there;
I just know you must be
truly hurting;
In excruciating pain for
which any salve I've tried
to apply failed. You are
lost without direction. The
maps I've thrown you
must be wrong.
For you are still not home.
The turmoil and distorted
thinking have traveled
from you to me.
I'm feeling it.
I'm empty, twisted inside.
What can I do to save you?
Can I save you? Can you
somehow feel my words?
Somewhere? They are
trying to lead you home.

I think I accidentally gave you
the defective map in utero.
I'm a lousy navigator.

Silence

Frank discussions over
broken plates and piece
meal lives,

"Is she badly designed?"

"No she's God's child too,
our child."

"What God?" I ask.

"Ask him for strength.
That's what he gives, not
miracle fixes."

My husband the
accountant,
pfftt,
what would he know of
God?

Who here on earth has
seen God, met him, talked
with him personally?

"But if he's all that,
why can't he perform
miracles? I hear he's
supposed to. I've prayed,"
I say.

100

"Look, I don't profess to
have all the answers; talk
to a minister."

I forgo that idea and
instead, take it back to the
top.

"God," I ask," Where are
you when I need you? "

Silence

*Do moms and daughters,
fathers and sons,
speak different languages?
Yes and yes*

Daddy's Girl

*A beautiful try at a poem by
her dad*

Sweet first child, so filled
with spunk,

What an athlete you were,
catching balls like a pro as
a toddler!

Your gifts so plentiful:
soccer, softball, A1 pitcher,
basketball, dog handler,
stepdancer, oh what fun
we had! After all, I am
your dad.

Then came the pain. You
thought you were fat,
developed eating issues,
friend issues, life issues.
You rode the totem pole
down to the bottom and as
you slipped down, a
monster grew.

Deadly friends, drugs,
cursing, stealing, fighting,
hitting. You hated me.
Wished me dead.

Our family was good.
What happened?
Soon you were kicked out,
cops came repeatedly; you
went missing for weeks. I
died inside wondering
about your safety. How
could I parent the others,
be a good husband?
I couldn't. I tried.

The stress took its toll.
When I couldn't sleep
night after night,
wondering if you were
dead or alive, when my
anxiety reached its peak,
when I felt the shame,
guilt, stress, sadness every
day, I wondered if I'd get
through, we'd get through.

But the light has peaked
around the clouds. The
rays are beginning to
shine. You are alive, you
have begun anew, you are
making positive choices,
you are living.
And you are forgiven and
loved.

The Next Chapter:
Hope and Life

*I'll carry your heart with me
in my backpack,
and as I wander and walk,
I'll feel your love tickling my
spine.*

Peace

To achieve true serenity

Cast away rage

Fling away loathing

Release sadness

Cull boredom

Reel in chocolate

Adversity

Adversity is like a glacier.
It's cold, hard to climb
over,
and knocks you back to
the bottom when you get
close to the top.
Take out your ax, and put
on your crampons. Don't
let a hunk-a-frozen water
win.

*Understanding a teenager is
like understanding quantum
physics.
You just don't.*

I Believe In You

Monster face fear
The doubt explodes
Too much to bear
On overload
Just take today
And make it shine
Then think of joy
You will be fine

Rejoice in your strength
Smile at the breeze
Breathe in fresh grass
A pollen fresh sneeze
Hold true to yourself
Let fear fall away
You've got this, my girl
In life you will stay

Take a lesson from your dog
Don't worry, be happy

Break Free

When you feel your back
against the wall,

Try to appreciate the cool
wood on your back and
the smooth feel of the
panel,

Then push the hell
through it to enjoy the
open space

*I'm so proud of the woman
you are becoming. I see
maturity developing before
my eyes, and as my eyes
water, my heart floats.*

Snare

Matches create infernos.

Beans grow to beanstalks.

Atoms cause explosions,

and spiders eat two
headed purple snakes.

See what little things can
do?

Now stop thinking, " I
can't," and go snare your
giant.

Be your own horse.
Treat yourself well,
and give yourself the ride of
your life.

Perfume

Wisps of perfumed
flowers
fall upon my senses,
as if trying to saturate my
suffering with sandalwood
rain and sprinkles of
musk,
or maybe just to awaken
the joy within reach.

Scattered petals
each a suffering soul,
Set adrift by someone who
cast their exquisiteness aside.

They say there is strength in
numbers, but sometimes true
grit is found in the courage to
remove ourselves from the
pack.

Ripple Effect

Ripples of emotion

keep extending out

Far reaching or surpassing

The edges of our doubt

Yes, were all connected

by an energetic fields

You exhale your atoms

then I inhale your yield

Kindness, love,
compassion

will reach another soul

If you toss it in the force
field

and watch the ripples
go.............

Be Yourself

Have you ever seen a
sunrise from another point
of view?

Looking from above it
makes it seem a bit askew,

But I've never seen such
beauty
In all my waking days

I think there is a lesson
here, to look for different
ways:

To appreciate variance

To seek new ways of
understanding

To love what's in front of
us, (even if there is a ring
in her nose)

To celebrate uniqueness

Carry On

Do you think today is
endless when tomorrow
never comes?

And yesterday is way too
late to make it right again?

Don't be fooled by night's
dark cast, the pall that
coats your world,

It's within you, my child,
the strength to change
the hope to carry on.

*Never be so serious that you
can't sometimes laugh at
yourself*

Stories

Some unwritten,
Some written then burned,
Some written then torn
and stomped on,
Some written the sold out
on,
Some written then
rewritten,
Some written then killed,
Some written then
blemished,
Some not even pondered,
not even born,
Stories
Our stories
Your stories
Which one are you?
Yours, my dear, is a bit of
them all, but the final
chapter is awaiting your
lead.

Rave

Shall we spread our wings
to dance semi naked in the
vast field of loneliness?
Show our vulnerability
while gaining strength?
I say we shall.
For in time, others will join
us, and we will realize we
all crave acceptance, that
we are not alone. And
soon our vulnerable solo
dance will turn into a rave.

*What storm awaits you
today? You DO have the
strength to go through it.*

Ne'er

Ne'er was there ever a star
so bright,
rising over amber fields
and lush greens.
No.
Ne'er was there ever a star
so damn beautiful, filling
the sky with hopes and
dreams and cotton candy
wishes.

Sigh, I'm smiling.

Ne'er was there ever a day
that I felt
such spectacular sparklets
of happiness creeping back
into my soul,

for you girl, are finally
seeking the sun

Fertilize

Take your ideas child,

and give them wings,

and whilst flying,

sprinkle a bit of your
blood, sweat and tears on
others

so your perspiration will
grow inspiration

and fertilize a garden of
eager minded seedlings.

*For those who love deeply
have hearts that bleed
profusely.
Those who don't love needn't
bother with band aids.*

Bible

Genesis, Exodus, Samuel,
Kings,

Chronicles, numbers,
verses and things.

A challenge by my
daughter to write about
God,

her faith ten times mine,
for that I applaud.

I skimmed through the
Bible looking for
inspiration,

but my hands were soon
soaked with uncertain
perspiration.

But I continued
laboriously, intent to finish
this task,

but saw such scary words,
this is the Bible I asked?

Words like plague,
blasphemy, crucify, death,

Gave rise to alarm,
Geeze, God makes me
sweat.

But continuing on with the
strength I'd been given,

gave rise to the words
unrelated to sinnen',

Compassion, salvation,
forgiveness of sins,

Maybe this God thing can
entice grins.

Hope and promises and
love everlasting,

even special oil used for
anointing,

My daughter's faithful
spirit, gifted me in a way,

that tear dropped my eye,
she and God moved me
today.

Torrid rain pounds my skin,
reminds me that I'm alive.

Come Out

When feeling forsaken and
standing in shadows,
defend your honor by
towering towards integrity
until the light of truth
shines.

For within our field of
vision is beauty well
within reach.
We just need to get out
from under that rock.

Lemonade

If I took the world's
lemons,
squeezed them all dry,
then added some sugar, no
one would cry,
because lemony sad things
should soon start to fade
and disappear fully from
sweet lemonade.

I love your smile
I love your soul
I love your words
I love you whole

Portals

If all of those corners,
of all those rough, tangled
edges of doubt continue to
stab into you,
and all those deep pockets
of poor judgment continue
to weigh you down,
just step through the
portal of strife and
uncertainty that surrounds
you,
and blast off to a new
world of hope.

Live

Suffice it to say, that the
deep agonizing moment
when you realize all hope
is gone and the freight
train that you expect for
years is finally barreling
down on you,
you give up.

Whistles shout, anxiety
climaxes, souls stir in a
horrible, "I'm dead way,"
and the echo of the
churning of the wheels is
so all consuming that your
brain atoms worry that
they will burst from the
negative energy reeling
full force inside them.

And then life stops…

Just for a moment….

Wheels cease, whistle
quiets, anxiety disappears.
Why?
Don't know;
but maybe because
somewhere in all that
nightmarish shit,

you have a spark of hope
that says......live.

*Pacifying peace will come
when you allow that restless
mind to slumber and let love
settle in.*

Heal

A hardened soul will repel
anything tossed at it:
words,
love,
compassion,
even darts.
A stoic shell grown of
misery and trial needs two
loving hands to massage
and hold, soften and bend,
to dissolve that poisonous
and unyielding force held
protectively dear.
Hold still, beautiful one,
and allow me to reach
within to touch and let the
healing begin.

Broken Love

Yes, my child, broken love
hurts in all the nooks and
crannies, places previously
unknown to the human
soul.

Each ripped shred of hope
backpacking home to its
place of residence before
the coffee sip smiles
and tentative kisses,
pounding crusty footsteps
deep and pulverizing into
the most tender recesses of
a once buoyant heart, now
dark with despair, now
covered watchfully with
memory's forlorn quilt.

But I'm so happy you can
once again feel.

Spears and Petals

And yes, life is damn hard
Every twist thrusts thorns,
Every turn spears swords,
But even as your feet bleed
crimson and the tears roll
down your sweet freckled
face, remember you also
walk amongst the petals of
daffodils
And the lone howl of
love's faithful song will
keep you company as it
echoes in the midnight
gloom.

Sing along, my sweet.

*You know I hate drugs. But
now I know they hate you. I
finally see them run! Good.*

Shoes

So many shoes to pick,
which will you choose?

The time worn leather of
the wise grandfather?

The pointy- feet ballerina
slippers to glide and sway
and twirl across the silken
stage?

Or perhaps you'll pick the
clunky metal toe hard-hat
shoe, to keep your fancy
feet safe from unseen
danger.

Or the Keds to play in, the
Jordans to jump in,
the fluffy slippers to hang
on the well worn couch.

Which shoes will you
wear?
You've those choices now.
Simple,
but representing life.

Layers

I was in our first home
years ago peeling layers
off the wall.
Layer
After
Layer
After
Layer
After
Layer
What I found beneath was
beautiful, a testimony to a
bygone time, a simpler
life, a time where painted
flower wallpaper was art,
and people sat on the
porch to talk whilst
looking each other in the
eye. There was depth to
the conversation because it
was about life, not iphones
or schedules or video
games. Fast forward a
hundred years. I do see
layers today- on onions, on
children bundled up in the
cold, on cakes.
But I don't see depth,
beauty perhaps, but not
depth. But you my child
have surprised me. You've

allowed me to peel off
your layers slowly to
discover things about you
that were hidden
treasures, each layer
revealed a bit more of a
soul so deep I still haven't
seen its end. You are full
of promising layers, all
treasures to be discovered,
all layers that hold more
then I could possibly hold.

*And as you write your new
chapter and wander with
scholars, may God hold your
hand and lead you to the
right classroom.*

Bloom

Did you ever see a wilted
flower?
Think of the joy and the
beauty it brought the first
time it was alive and
vibrant:
the smell,
the colors,
the joy,
the peace.
That's you, sweet child.
You are my flower, but
there is no reason to wilt.
I am sorry if I neglected to
water you.
I'm sorry if I didn't feed
your soul. You are what
brings color to my life, and
I promise to nourish you
every day.
I am just a beginning
gardener, but I want to
tend to you and watch you
bloom.

Knock Me Out

Thump, thump
Sharp bricks falling
Boom, boom,
Hit me again
Down on knees
Prayers unanswered
Ha, ha
Taunt me instead

Icons shatter, the false
gods haunt,
Hopes and dreams dive
fast
Edges strike me sharply
now
Knock me out at last

Brick and mortar raining
down
The tremors moving quick
Temple of doom collapses
on me
Vomit wakes me warm
and thick

Then enter sunshine,
strength, and trust
The tools of love to build,
My vomit dries, cathedral
rises, with happiness it's
filled.

Shelters me from stormy
night; it feeds my empty
shell.
My new safe haven holds
me tight,
My sanctuary from hell.

*May the morning sun greet
you kindly
May the gentle breeze rustle
your hair
May the beauty of the day
allow you to breathe
May you appreciate the gifts
right in front of you*

Song

Chirping birds fill the air
this Sunday
Their sweet hymn of
devotion mesmerizes me
So alive in song
They can only be crooning
abut you
Their joy lifting my spirits,
now I'm singing too.

Dusk veiled in black,
Sun takes a back seat
heading to her own funeral
where night will officiate.
May she be resurrected
tomorrow

Vultures

And on my walk…

Amidst the kettles of
vultures, two eyes watch,
flocks soak up vitamin D,
tanning wings, committees
form on rooftops to
discuss today's gourmet
decay. Mating dances,
preying waltzes,
offer music to a mortal's
morning bath.
Carry on, on carrion, Mr.
Vulture.
Carry on indeed.
And thank you for my
bird's eye view,
a humble first for me.

*In the midst of healing from
despair,
Remember to appreciate the
simplicity of a walk and its
wonders.*

Tilted

Today is better, a sunny
day blossoming after my
heart had been a tilt a
whirl,
spinning out of control,
threatening to spill me
onto the filthy pavement,
leaving open wounds,
inviting more infected
thoughts to invade my
fragile being.
I asked God to stop the
ride.
It did stop.
And today is beautiful.

*I allow calm waters to carry
me to horizon's unknown,
passing rainbows and sunsets
as I go. I bask in the delight
of earthly surprises and find
joy in the waters below.*

The Healing Cover

Comfy cozy covers are a

nice place to hide

From life

From pain

From stress

From hopelessness

Mmmmmmm

It's lovely under here.

But I smell coffee,

inhale the aroma hard.

And I'm going to drink

it too.

So I place my feet on the

floor and move.

So there comfy, cozy

covers!

Take that!

**I bequeath thee covers to someone else who needs a break. Give them respite please.
I'm getting on with my life.**

When feeling forsaken and standing in shadows, defend your honor by towering toward integrity until the light of truth shines.

Travel is my Peace

Memories hit of majestic
mountains and moonlit
passages illuminating holy
shrines.
Oh, the beauty!
The tastes of potent reds in
vineyards under verandas,
Gaudi inspired
perplexities, a whimsical
visionary enjoyed with
seafood paella and wine.
My heart bleeds for more!
Bejeweled shafts of light
beckon again from
imposing cathedrals of
stone. I'm coming soon!
Sumptuous colors of busy
bazaars offer the strange,
the lovely, and the, "I'll
never, ever, taste that."
My need to be a gypsy
with holes in my shoes
and wonder in my gaze,
does not coexist with my
need for simplicity, a
homey sanctuary, a
thatched roof cottage,
simple, with a Guinness
on the table and a sheep in
the yard. Maybe it's
merely a function of my

dysfunction, or maybe it's
just me.

*Go, just go, Mom, Dad. Don't
wait for your miracle or you'll
be missing your life too. The
drug doesn't care, is glad to
keep you grounded and
afraid. Go and explore the
world; let go of the fear and
embrace your life and your
wanderlust for a week. You'll
be glad you did.*

Mother

Written by another daughter,
my Molly

To my mother
With eyes like river water
Hair like flames
Dark dotted stars on her
porcelain skin
Who has walked the
realms of hell
Watching her daughter
run with the devil
Witnessing eternal love in
marriage
Burn to ashen flames
before her
To my mother
who locks away her scars
In a chest no one has
found
Or will ever find
Because she safeguards it
with smiles
And endless compassion
Hairspray and lipstick,
small talk and housework,
To my mother
whose words are soothing
water
On many foreign
wounded hearts

Who speaks casualties
through her lips
Then writes down the
universe with her pen
To my mother
who has felt the words in
the wind
Secrets in the soil
Concepts in the treetops
Sculpting them into poems
that have rippled hearts
Across the sea
To my mother
who will never know her
own worth
Under her lemon juice
stained skin
finger pinched stomach
Mascaraed eyes
Who speaks beauty
Who is beauty
For she is God's perfect
image
A creation a billion years
in the making until it was
her time
To be sent to the universe
To change my world
forever
Who continues to change
the world
Sending words into the
universe

Words responsible for the
sun
That beams on my cold
face
Wind on my heated back
Moss under my aching
feet
To my mother
who is loved more than
she knows
Or will ever know
Because she is beautiful
She is a masterpiece

Colors

Another by the masterful
Molly

All of the colors I see in
the wind
That paint the treetops and
jagged cliffs
Were formed from a
woman
With skin of Maplewood
And I have learned much
about home
Finding and losing it
In the illusion of a journey
About shifting phases
Shifting people
Shifting time to make me
grow older
And when I have
I realized
That love has a limit
Bone bound in some
people
That love cannot be
written in sparking jump
ropes or little queens,
But can live in the wings
of a butterfly
Every movement of its
wing propelling
handcrafted molecules
into the air

Like a dance
It moves on
Like life
Like the scars of time
And the surrounding
protective tissue it learns
to grow
Like remembering the
rippling waters
Of a village kingdom
where wood skin used to
flourish
Realizing that time was
wrong
The past is incorrect
Only the present bares
truth
So take a walk in a
pebbled pond
Seek heaven not on its
reflective surface
But on the muddy bottom
Where many things that
have died now live

A daughter is a gift
A daughter with compassion
is a rare gift
A daughter who survived a
rough journey due to another
Is one in a million
And still, you smile

Cold

Another by my Molly

I know you're cold
I know your heart has
been frosted with ice
I know your smiles are old
ones, from years ago
They froze on your face
when the snow came in
And slaughtered the
warmth
I know you've searched
for love
Only to visit its grave days
later, icicles suspended at
its stone sides
I've seen you shed tears of
ice
Seen the cold winds born
from your laughter
Felt the shivering of your
broken lungs
You have braved the
snowstorm
And it has passed above
our heads
But still resides within you
So just remember
When you feel your toes
and fingers go numb
That I am thinking fondly
of you

That I wish only sunshine
upon your pale face
Blooming daisies in your
smile
Birdsong in our heart
For you were molded by a
million meadows
That cast away glaciers
And I will cast the cold
away too
If you allow me
Because I love you

Humanity

I believe in the
brotherhood
and sisterhood of
humanity
Humanhood, I'd call it
I crave it
Dearly
Where all races
All creeds
All religions
All sexes
All sexual orientations
All humanity
Come together as one
Unfortunately, that's not
what I see today.
I see
too many people fighting
their agendas
Based on race
Based on religion
Too many people with
blinders on ignoring the
truth because it doesn't fit
their purpose
Too many fools profiting
from racial crime
Ignoring their own killing
their own
or one religion killing
another

Or one sex enslaved and
hidden from sight
I love God's human
garden
Beauty in all its
possibilities
But sometimes I wish we
were all green and talked
the same and believed the
same and were
programmed the same
For just one day
So those that believe that
"brotherhood" or
"sisterhood "is of only
their choosing...
Their race better
Their sex better
Their ideas better... would
be bored as hell,
twiddling their thumbs
from the madness of a sea
of puke green
The one way
conversations
The sexlessness
The roboticness
The boredom
A dull landscape of
Stepford humans
Soon they'd be begging for
a change
But,

no one would profit
Monetarily
Egotarily
Controlitarily
Sexually
from exploiting another
different
I wish some ugly hearted
people would cut the
bullshit. And return to
grace,
To humanhood
We all crave acceptance
We all bleed red
Give your neighbor a hug
Find out his differences
and discover his
similarities
And be thankful
You're not both green
And smile because you are
part of God's intricate
garden
And he picked you to
decorate a special part of
it.

True creativity allows one artist's view to be seen differently through the eyes of another, both beautiful, both true.

Death to the Inquisitor

No more must I be the
inquisitor,
the parental intelligentsia
scooping up top secret
information by way of
three party phone calls
and Facebook searches.
No more must I be the one
with a mommy warrant,
searching for whatever
drug paraphernalia you've
exiled.
No more must I be the
symbolic exorciser, an evil
shooing priest purging
you of whatever devil lies
within. No more must I
worry, though of course I
still do, but still, no more
must I cry myself to sleep,
blanketed by my own
frightful shivers.
I can breathe.
Finally, no more.

16 Hours

For 16 hours you've been
up…in a good way,
bopping your blonde head
around college classrooms
and workplaces.

For 16 hours you've been
interacting with the world,
absorbing knowledge,
offering your wonderful
gifts to clients and friends.

For 16 hours you've lived
your exhausting life fully.

Remember when 16 hours
was hell?

I do.
But no more,
because you are
stronger than Lucifer.

The Son

*And meanwhile as I try to
parent my other kids…*

Today I told him that love
hurts like hell,
can twist a gut into shapes
not known possible.

I heard him cry yesterday
for the first time in years,
heart wrenching, stomach
spasming sobs.

Hours later he came to me.

"Mom, what can I do to
change, to show her I'll
grow up, respect her, and
be a real man?"

First Kiss

And my daughter….

Giddy laugh trembles
excitedly,
dancing in the light,
refreshing air,
surrounding a budding
young woman's blushing
glow.
Breaths of fresh
tomorrows skip rope on
hopeful dreams.
Her first kiss didn't
disappoint.
The sparkle in her eyes
said it all.
She found a piece of
heaven whilst alive, at
least for a moment.
And she smiles,
oh how she smiles.

*Take the time to appreciate
your other kids*

Angel

I felt the feathered touch of
silken hands,
the whispered comfort of a
beautiful woman in white,
the envelopment of my
soul...that awful day.
I imagined her wings
fluttering softly as she
lifted me after a miserable
attempt to pray, when
hope's uncertain burden
crushed me to blubbering
pulp. Somehow, still, I felt
something beautiful, and
my tears stopped as hope
changed from burden to
dream, and the goodness
of a mysterious unknown
granted me a day of peace,
a glimmer of faith's
shining light.

Garden

God built a garden
Or somehow a garden was
built
A cosmic collision from
nothing
Or a spiritual construction
I don't care how it was
born
But it's beautiful
These colors and flavors of
humanity
Meant to be cherished,
discovered,
shared, and loved.
And a few jackass
advocates for the devil
won't bring down the
strong,
the united,
the high moral character of
the masses.
God bless our children
and the communities that
raise them together.

Lonely Child

Outside the crickets sing a
beautiful song,
more welcome than the
thunderous rains of
yesterday.
And somewhere a child
lies on a bed, a sofa, a
chair,
not knowing his worth,
feeling forlorn and alone,
shades of doubt and
distress scratching his
heart.
"Do I matter?" he
wonders.
And a spider spins its
silky web under waning
moon, as a tired Black Lab
scratches a linoleum floor.
And not far away, though
millions of miles, another
lonely soul hugs a beat up
pillow, hoping, praying,
for a friend.

*Reach out and touch a sad
life.*

Tomorrow

When tomorrow comes:

I promise to extinguish
your fears with love's
grace.

I promise to allow your
hair to tickle my nose as
you rest your tired head
on my shoulder.

I promise to nourish your
needy soul with freely
gifted compassion.

I promise to love you *just
as you are.*

Seeking

And does the water's edge
hold love's propensity?
Yes, dear one.
Harmonious secrets wash
up and glisten within
molten sand,
held by Mother Nature's
grace,
then gifted absolution
back to watery hearth-
God's psalm,
man's cherishment, life's
shape shifting hope,
love...
adrift and alive,
seeking....seeking

Alien Love

There are hearts that beat
only to make it through
life, a quiet lazy song
accompanying human
sloth.
Then there are those that
fill the chest of their
owners.
I see them every day: the
givers, energetic souls
lost in their selfless
unimportance.
They paint the
masterpieces of human
kindness,
colorful life canvasses
auctioned off freely to lift a
desperate soul.
Then there are those hearts
that can't contain their
own worth, like yours,
because their worth is
unknown even to
themselves. Extraordinary
goodness bleeds and
bubbles over, then
eventually rises to join
atmospheric nothingness,
saturating it with the same
love gifted others, and as it
lifts beyond infinity, I can't

help but think that light
years away, a crippled
misunderstood being is
being healed from the
misty risen goodness
of you.

Tell Her

Every moment
we are reminded that we
are not promised the
precious rays of day break.
So today, tell her she's
beautiful.
Today, tell him you love
him.
Today, do something
exciting for yourself. And
as the sun continues to
rise,
warm the earth,
and set,
we can bet life goes on.
And if unfortunately we
cease to exist in this life, at
least we know we died
trying to live.

"You are beautiful."

Discombobulated

I don't like feeling lost,
discombobulated, unsure.
As life would have it,
I do.
But if the straightest lane
had been laid out before
me,
and I decided to skip
down its clear and concise
path,
I wouldn't have gained the
strength needed to love
you.
I wouldn't have felt the
rousing stab of unexpected
thorns, wouldn't have
smelled the disturbing
pungency of defeat,
wouldn't have risen
stronger, resolute.
Life is not about the easy
path. It's about the razor
sharp, disquieting
moments that make you
bleed.
It's about the bandages
that make you heal.
It's about the scabs that
make you durable.
For only from those
inelegant gifts,

do we really appreciate
the occasional rose.

*Did I tell you how proud I am
of your recovery? Well, I am.
You've more strength then
ten thousand soldiers, for I
now understand the pull of
drugs. Damn, Girl, you are
amazing.*

Mask

I know who you are
Under there
The barbed mask you
wear can't hide it; the
truth that's been drowned
by experience's
devastating executioner.
But I still know who you
are.
You see? Look there.
Those bubbles that surface
from your drowning are
the colors of truth's
rainbow, alive with
promise; and your soulful
eyes still shine with hope
in the face of adversity's
hangman.
And even when you feel
like the crushed bone
dinner of the devil himself,
you fight, and I see
strength and beauty filter
up through the choking
black, a faith restoring
lava, covering, covering,
covering the sad,
depressing, and fearful

until they're buried
beneath the glow of the
gladiator within.
For no one, NO ONE
should get you down.
Because you are beautiful;
you are strong; you are
thankfully unique, and
you are a gift to those who
love you,

and I know who you are.

*And today hope is born
Conceived of joy
and the promise of light
Bury its woeful afterbirth,
for horizon calls to guide you
forth*

Feel it

Have you ever been really
scared?

Cry out in the night, bite
down on your tongue
scared?

Lost and alone, mixed up
in your head scared?

Where is he, what is he
doing scared?

Is she alive, hurt, or in
trouble scared?

How can I possibly get
through one more day
scared?

I have,
you have,
we all have,
they all have…
been scared.

And it's cotton picken'
lousy.
Miserable.
Horrible.
Soul searing.

Rip roaring bad.

Feel it.

It's ok.
You're strong. It's ok
It's ok.
It is ok

This flow of salty fluid echoes
with hollow emptiness
Yet the corners of my eyes
overflow, filled beyond
capacity.

Space

You asked me about space
in a way I hadn't thought.
I expected to try to turn
Copernicus on his head or
throw Galileo through a
black hole.
I'd thought I'd stretch my
mind to the farthest limits
of the unknown, hoping
for a revelation, a peek
into understanding the not
understandable, fighting
brain straining implosion
as I found some sort of
awareness to a perfectly
placed puzzle, bound by a
limitless, ever-changing
frame.
But you ask of space
between people and what
to fill it with. Don't you
already know the answer
to that? Love, sweet child,
the answer is simply love.

Love is the ultimate medicine,
better than cod liver oil. By
far. Take a few teaspoons.

Petal

If I were to place a petal in
your hand, would you
release it in the wind to fly
on soft air?

Or would you carry it
tenderly between the soft
round of your thumb and
the tender caress of your
palm?

Would you press it gently
between Dickens and
Whitman to dry with
memories we have
shared?

Or would you set it atop a
shelf to be seen, a
reminder of our
relationship, our beauty?

What would you do with
it, love? You see, I've
planted a garden of hope
with seeds of your grace,
and it is you, my dear,
who will gift me a
thousand blossoms.

One tender petal, one soft
silken fragile bit, will
forever hold the richest
treasure imaginable. A
little bit of us.

Barnes and Noble

And on the home front…

Her disquiet unnerves me,
throws me back to another
daughter and her hell.
Leathery hands, slick oil
sweat drape her face, sick
puppy pants, she needs to
get out.
Now.
"I'm going crazy," she
murmurs.
I contemplate doctors,
psychiatrists,
anything to calm her
nerves.
But instead she guides me
to the solution.
Five bucks and a lift to
Barnes and Noble, where
she sits and writes day in
and day out, a masterpiece
forming under the deft
fingers of a 16 year old
panic stricken genius.
I gladly pay for her lattes.
It's a hell of a lot cheaper
than therapy, and it
returns me with a huge
teenage smile.

Sometimes in the midst of a child's addiction, a parent forgets to be the best parent possible to the others. 'Forgets' might be an incorrect word. Let's say 'tries, but fails.' Parenting others in the midst of a storm is quite a feat. Forgive me if I've failed, I can only hope what you've learned from the experience makes up for it.

Faces with Names

There are faces
behind the disease. Loved
faces.
Faces with names like
Justin, Michael, Debbie,
Josh, and Mark.
Beautiful faces once filled
with hope and promise
and a wide open future.
Faces loved by their
parents,
their kids,
their friends.
Dark faces.
Light faces.
Long faces.
Round faces.
Faces created from love,
then cherished and
groomed and guided and
kissed.
Faces who did what all of
us have done at one time
or another.
Made a mistake.
Faces who have felt like
we have.
Insecure.
Not good enough.
Scared.
Sad.

Overwhelmed.
Human faces.
Imperfect faces.
Faces representing every
damn child in America.
Beautiful faces faced with
hard choices.
To fit in.
To look cool.
To erase pain.
Faces attached to good
hearts,
Giving faces
Faces who didn't know
their susceptibility to a
substance greater than
their will.
Faces that didn't know
they'd soon be under an
evil spell.
Faces that couldn't fight
anymore.
Faces that left their loved
ones with just memories.
Faces that now represent
a fight to save other faces
who too are struggling,
who too have loving
families,
who too didn't know the
power of the devil, who
too have hope to live.

Thank you Justin, Michael,
Debbie, Mark, and Josh for
gracing us with your lives
and for starting a deeply
needed conversation.
Your faces
Your souls
Your spirits
Your grace
will never be forgotten.

*God save our children. And if
you're not really there,
someone please save our
children.*

Remote

I press on the bruised skin
of the remote, hoping for
relief, a trip to Mars or the
dusty wilds of the
pyramids, perhaps a
stomp around a climatic
mystery would do; but I'm
still here, sitting on stained
cushions, tiptoeing around
my mind's magnanimous
seesaw of doubt, waiting
for a call from the straight
A student, softball pitcher
who once danced an Irish
jig for her class and
hugged me close before
bedtime. I fiddle with the
remote, half crazed with
hope, half dead with
despair, and I ask myself
over and over, "Have I
saved you?"
Then the call comes,
"Hi, Mom. School was
great today, I got an A."
And I remember that I
didn't save you. I know
now that you have saved
yourself.

Optimism

Maybe I will forget the
past. Maybe time's cold
hand will do its job,
shaking each screaming
moment, each violent
episode, from my
memory,
pushing,
shoving,
each drug fueled snapshot
over the edge of my
remembrance until they all
come tumbling down,
free flying in midair,
smashing,
shattering,
flinging
all the old crap into
oblivion's eternal heaven.
Yes, maybe I will forget.
And your recovery and
optimism are allowing me
the hope that I will.

Truth

Truth.

Can hurt like hell.

Truth.

Can liberate.

Truth.

Can bring out a brave
side.

Truth.

Can destroy.

Truth.

Can cause
reconsideration.

Truth.

Can make us look inward.

Truth.

Can make us look
outward.

It's real.

It's honest.

It's naked.

It's harsh.

It's direct

It's true.

AND IT HEALS.

Don't be afraid of your own truth.

You'd be surprised at the support you'll receive when the disguise come off.

My truth is I wish I understood you more when you were a child. Your outbursts were terrible, and I thought you troubled, but perhaps you just needed a bit more of me.

Smoke

The soft tendrils of smoke
pirouette in the air, a
cancer laced dance,
breaking their
performance by taking
refuge in my throat as they
dig their sharp toes into
the tender red flesh inside.
I'm choking, drowning in
a sea of hazy Marlboro
emissions,
and I feel a disease begin,
waltzing with the skanky,
sooty reeking skirt and
sweater I now wear.
But I must accept,
must sit with the cryptic
fog in a dark room, must
keep quiet as my breath
becomes shallow and my
head becomes light.
After all, I am the mom
and I've come here to
learn.

Yes, I'd suffocate for you.

Goodbye Poison

The toxicity has left.
The spiraling thunderbolts
of electric madness have
quietly and quickly gone
away. One day it became
clear again, and the sun
burst through the clouds
like a ripped football
banner. One day the world
began again and the clock
started to move forward,
seconds, minutes, hours. I
noticed at the same time
how the moistened petals
of the rose opened and
gleamed, how the birds
sang songs of
indescribable sweetness,
how a baby's cry became
music to my ears. The day
the toxicity left, I started to
live. The day it left we
started a new journey
together.

Skipping Stones

Heaven must be a step
below this. It has to be. For
nowhere else could I feel
such intense joy and see
such deep beauty. The
rippling waters of the
Delaware lap my bare feet
as the old ship sails on by.
I'm here seeing this,
listening to the gulls,
skipping stones with my
youngest child, smelling
the luxurious aroma of
seaweed and a bit of trash.
But it's better than heaven,
because somewhere you
decided to live and
somewhere far away on
Earth's water's edge, you
are skipping stones too.

Gate

There upon the rusted
swinging gate sits a
redheaded child, her face
sprinkled with the kisses
of angels. Her torn sneaker
digs into a rusted bar, a
viable hope for stability. I
watch her unknowing
face, still innocent and
unaware of the challenges
she will face only a few
years from now. She
jumps off, snagging her
dress, tearing it away
without a care in the
world. As she skips
happily towards the lake,
the fresh smell of daisies
pierces my nostrils. I
breathe it in and cherish
this moment of bliss and
innocence. I don't want
that child to know the
dangers ahead of her. I
want her to keep smelling
the daisies and swinging
on rusted gates.

Jump

The deep red of the

parachute carved a lithe

design into the pale blue

of summer

sky's landscape.

I'd always thought them

crazy, you know the

type that risk their lives

for a thrill. Now I envy

them. After living in

life's darkest shadows, I

wish I'd the courage to

fly.

The Change

As steam escapes the
confines of its prior liquid
life,

And caterpillars change
their form to butterflies in
flight,

And snowy blankets melt
away to newly sodden
spring,

And rage filled storms
give way to rainbows only
God can bring;

A blond haired lass once
dark as night once
imprisoned and sedated,

Changes course and seeks
the light,
Finally liberated!

Living

A poem by her

Do you know what peace
feels like?

Real peace?

The kind of peace when
explosive volcanic magma
turns into igneous rock?

The silence of the land
when the waters recede
back into the sea after
swallowing it whole?

Calm after destruction?

Destruction that brings
you close to death

Yet you were already
dead... The walking dead?

Do you know what
resurrection feels like?

The pain of transforming
back into a living being?

The terrifying thoughts,
actions, feelings?

But then, the first time
noticing how blue the sky
is.
The birds in the trees, the
shapes of the clouds, the
scent of a flower.

Uninhibited beauty in all
its glory.

Do you know how it feels
to love, and be loved?

The kind of love after
years of isolation?

Throwing knives and
cannonballs at anyone
who dared to even come
close...

To opening up your soul?

To caring about the hearts
of others before your own,
and feeling satisfaction
and joy?

Do you know what its like
to live?

Really live?

The kind of loving after a
coma?

The relieving gasp of air
after drowning?

Taking in each moment
good and bad?

Feeling unconditional love
and sincere youthful
happiness?

Learning, growing,
feeling?

Appreciating each and
every moment on this God
given earth?

Tuning out the noise of life
and taking time to
appreciate the littlest of
things?

To be ever grateful?

Do you know what it's like
to love life?

To feel free?

I do.

And I know you can too.

You have life awaiting, an encyclopedia of new sunrises hoping to be discovered and admired, a future husband and children anticipating your arrival and theirs. Say goodbye to the stupid drug, for more important things will and CAN only be conceived by you. And they are oh, so worth it.

Horizon

I looked over at the amber
glow of the new moon as
it shined on the glistening
asphalt. A summer rain
had fallen, and the drops
of liquid lingered,
sparkling, a reminder that
jewels live here, in this
very house. I know you're
over there now, many
miles away, a wise
decision, given the
relapse rate of returning
addicts. As much as I miss
you, I know you are
better there, will carve out
a beautiful life. I know
that you have risen, as the
sun above a dreary
landscape, a moon above
a dark wooded path. You
have indeed risen, so I
name this book for your
resurrection my dear, so
proud of your rising. You
have come so far beyond
your fall. I love you.

My words

About the author

Maureen Alexandra Fitzpatrick resides in NJ with her family. She has 5 children and teaches online, as well as writes up a storm. She wants you to know you are not alone on this terrible walk. Look for the horizon and a fresh morning sunrise.

Made in the USA
Middletown, DE
27 August 2016